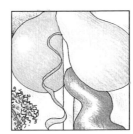

# Planning a party

## CONTENTS

# Introduction

A party is a celebration of something special. Parties bring family and friends together to share food and fun.

*Birthdays*

*Special occasions*

*Christmas*

Sometimes parties
are held for no
special reason.

'Things to do' list

Decide on a date, time and place

Invite the guests

Plan the food and fun activities

Make decorations

Prepare food

Greet your guests

Enjoy the party

Thank your guests

Clean up the party area

# Invitations

Talk about the party with your family.

Decide on the day, time and place for the party.

Plan the invitations. Make sure the guests are told everything they need to know.

## Circus invitations

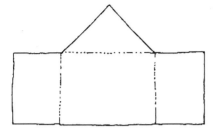 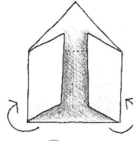 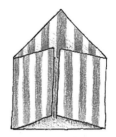

**1** Cut out the shape.  **2** Fold.  **3** Draw the stripes.

## Mask invitations

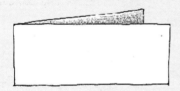 

**1** Fold a rectangle of cardboard 35 cm by 9 cm in half.

**2** Draw a mask outline.

**3** Write inside:

1 Cut out this mask.

2 Decorate it.

3 Wear it to the party.

You are invited to Tilak's party on Saturday 24th October from 2 pm to 4.30 pm. Place: 27 Park Road, Mulberry Green RSVP 0123 87654

# Decorations

Simple decorations help to create a special party feeling.

Make decorations for the table, door and ceiling.

Party hats are decorations too.

**BEFORE . . .**

**AFTER . . .**

Decorations can be made from:

- newspaper
- coloured paper
- aluminium foil
- balloons
- bin liners
- garden netting
- coloured streamers

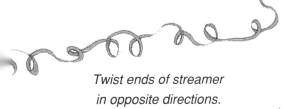

Twist ends of streamer
in opposite directions.

Join pieces of different
coloured streamers to
make a chain.

Cut shapes in bin liners
and attach across windows.

## Pirate hats

You will need:
black cardboard
white paper
scissors
glue
stapler

(1) Cut black cardboard
into pirate hat shape.

(2) Cut skull and crossbones
out of white paper.

(3) Paste them on to the hat
shape and staple ends to
fit around your head.

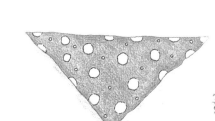

Tie a spotted scarf
around your head.

# Party food

Planning party food is a lot of fun. Decide on several
different kinds of food.

Choose your favourite food. Choose other foods that
are colourful and delicious. Make the food look
exciting by:

- cutting special shapes
- arranging it in special ways
- putting brightly coloured foods together.

Jelly and ice-cream are great party foods. Special biscuits and cakes are fun to make and serve. Make two lists.

Before Saturday

jelly oranges

animal biscuits

cup cakes

chocolate crispies

meatballs

falafel

On Saturday

sandwiches, pittas, pizzas

vegetable kebabs

popcorn

fruit punch

ice-cream clowns

Mini pizzas

Funny face sandwiches

Garden bugs

Falafel

Potato boats

10

## Vegetable kebabs

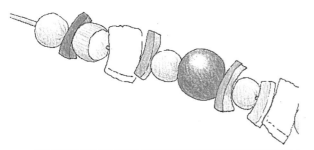

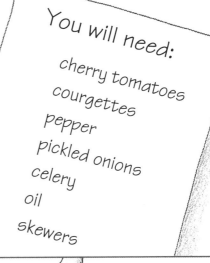

You will need:

cherry tomatoes
courgettes
pepper
pickled onions
celery
oil
skewers

**1** Cut the vegetables into large pieces.

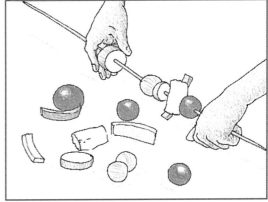

**2** Thread the vegetables on to a skewer.

**3** Brush with oil.

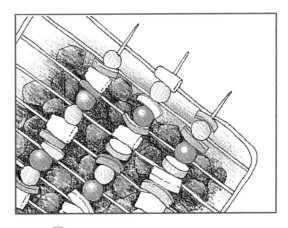

**4** Grill or barbeque until vegetables are browned.

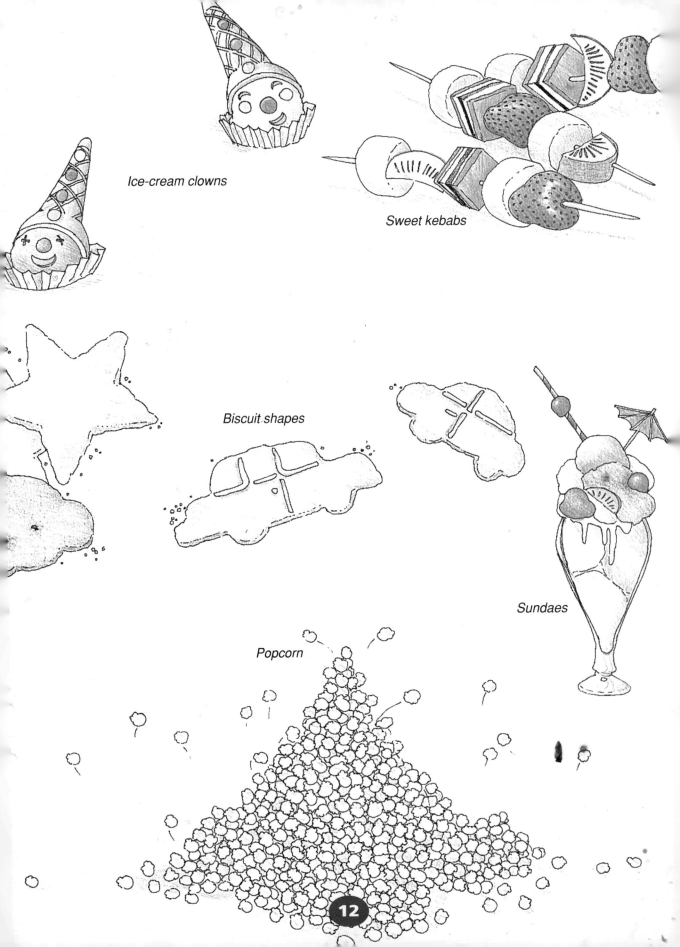

Ice-cream clowns

Sweet kebabs

Biscuit shapes

Sundaes

Popcorn

12

**Jelly oranges**

You will need:
oranges
1 packet of jelly
boiling water
trays

**1** Cut oranges in half. Scoop out all the flesh without breaking the skin.

**2** Place skin bowls on trays. Secure with Blu-Tack.

**3** Make jelly with 250 ml of boiling water. Pour into skin bowls.

**4** Refrigerate until set. Cut each bowl in half and serve.

# Party games

Play party games before and after eating. Choose games that will make people laugh. It is not important who wins these games. Ask someone to take photos of the fun.

Musical hats

Balloon score

## Treasure hunt

(1) Hide the items to be found, around your house or garden.

(2) Make a list of the items on each paper bag.

(3) Give the bags to guests.

(4) Set a time to collect the items.

(5) Give prizes for collecting all the items.

a small stone

a piece of newspaper

an empty crisp packet

two kinds of leaves

a teaspoon

# Theme parties

Choose a theme for the party. Make decorations, hats, food and games to fit in with the theme.

Princess theme

Pirate theme

Circus theme

Space theme

net curtain

17

# After the party

Thank the guests as they leave.  You might be
able to give them a treat as well.

Help clean up the room after the party. Take down the decorations. Put the furniture back in its usual place. Thank your family for helping you give a great party.

# Index